Cover artwork by Kenny Durkin

All caricatures by Kenny Durkin

Editing by Ann Harmer, Bluff Hollow Editing Services

To: Lisa! welcome
to reunion resort
JAN - 2013

ACKNOWLEDGMENTS

It is never possible to mention everyone who guided and inspired me to write this book, so I'll start by apologizing to those I've left out here, and to thank these folks who have been special in my life.

I must thank Doris Byrd, my dear friend; Chef Michael Ha, the best sushi chef in the world; Bev Kelber, Jay Rocha and all the members and wonderful staff at Reunion Resort.

I must thank my dear family, the KGB clan (our family-reunion acronym that includes the family names Keown and Bivins), most of whom are in Kentucky. Bonnie, you have inspired me to be who I am—thank you!

This second book, *The Evolution*, is dedicated to my late grandmother, Pearl Bivins; my late mom, Micheal Keown Coons; my dad, Bill Coons; my late brother Gary Lee, and my niece Mary Ann Lee.

Mom says we need to get on it and get Book 2, The Evolution, under way! So here we go. After we finished the first book, Mom went on a cruise with her good friend Karen Reynolds. Something happened to Mom on that trip—not sure what, but she says it was the Caribbean air and perhaps the Caribbean rum! After she left St. Maarten, she definitely started the Evolution journey.

The Evolution story began with a dolphin. My mom went through a very difficult personal struggle in 1999, which I know little about because I wasn't around yet. I met her in 2002, and by that time much of the initial pain had passed. However, I could sense her pain, which lay deep inside her. So when I met her on the curb that day at the Winter Park Farmers Market, I knew I was supposed to go home with her! Fortunately for me, my man was selling my three brothers and me because he needed money to move. You see, I was a bit of what they call a rescue. The man who owned my birth mom was in desperate need of cash for moving expenses, and today Mom says, "Thank God for ATMs!"

I fell in love with my mom that day, and she took me home!

Anyway, back to the dolphin story. Mom says the first item she placed in her new house, after dealing with the loss and pain she had been going through for over a year, was a statue of a dolphin, which she named Evolution. She said this was the symbol she needed to move on. She identifies dolphins with fun and freedom, and she found freedom from pain and some fun when she went though this change in life. However, she was caught up in a growing business—land and home acquisitions—and her lifestyle was very stressful. Many of the anecdotes in this little book reflect my reasons for writing it.

AND this is the why the term Evolution is so significant!

Oh yeah, back to the cruise, which was in March. I stayed home and took care of things. I love my dog-sitters, but I would rather have Mom home. All my life she has traveled for work and leaves me! She sure tries hard, though, and finds some pretty cool people to stay with me. Doris is my favorite house-sitter, but Mom has to get a dog-walker when Doris stays with me, as I am too strong for Doris. One time when Doris was watching me while Mom played golf, I saw a dog in the backyard and pulled Doris down. I felt so bad because the fall broke her arm. Poor Doris! She waited until Mom was finished with her golf game before she did anything about it. Doris just had a beer and waited . . . so Doris ended up in the doctor's office and came out with a sling! No more dog-walking with Doris!

Oh yeah, back to Mom's Evolution.

Mom says she was beginning to feel very stressed, and the economic times had killed her business. I have been with her for ten years, moved with her three times and watched her struggle to make it. She tried so hard to manage all the properties she owned, travel all the time for the business AND take care of me and Tigger. I could see the stress in her body, and it scared me! I watched her deal painstakingly with all this, and I was really worried. Then something extraordinary happened. In July, after Mom got back from her motorcycle trip to Michigan, her friend Ruth came to visit while looking for a job in Orlando. Ruth and my mom went to have sushi at Chef Ha's sushi bar in Reunion. Whenever Mom goes to eat sushi, she comes home in a better mood. She says she hangs out with lots of good friends and meets a lot of new people who visit and stay at the resort. Some of the characters at Reunion are just what the doctor ordered for her mental health. She always seems more relaxed and happy when she comes home from the sushi bar.

So that Wednesday night in July was no different! But of course when she got home, she had to tend to me and take me for my walk. It was dark, so we didn't take our usual route through the tunnel and to the Villas. Instead, we turned right and walked through our neighborhood. This crazy little "ball-of-fur" dog was out and started yapping at me. I had had enough of this little guy and charged the rascal!

My poor mom was holding on, and down she went! Ruth was in the house, and Mom said her shoulder was really hurting! So Ruth, who is a nurse, put some ice in a Ziploc bag, and my mom put it on her collarbone. She fell asleep on the couch around 10 pm. So, around 5 am, we all woke up in the living room. Mom got up to go upstairs, realizing she had appointments that day, and in the most unreal way, fell flat on the tile floor! This woke up our friend, Ruth the nurse, and she asked my mom if she was okay. Well, of course my mom said, "Yeah, I think so." She picked herself up and went for the stairs, but fell again. Nurse Ruth said, "Are you sure you're okay?" My mom said, "Sure," then got up and walked again to the stairs. This time she fell down, hit her head square on the tile floor and knocked herself completely out.

Now just to be clear, this part of the story will have its the ending later in the book, because this is the main event that stirred up the Evolution, the inspiration for this book. You see, we learned later that a condition had developed when my mom fell while walking me earlier that night, which I explain a bit later. Geez, do I feel bad, yep . . . but not so much, as the Evolution came to fruition because of what happened on a night in July of

2011.

Okay, my mom wants me to tell the story about why she went on this wine and sushi craze in the first place. I promise it won't be too long, as I have to take a break and go for treats and bathroom breaks, okay?

Mom says this whole thing began when she was watching a movie, "The Castaway," with Tom Hanks. She loves movies and is a movie buff, but this one resonated in a different way than most. Since the character Tom Hanks played was stranded on an island after a plane crash, my mom began thinking how this could happen to her. She traveled so much for work the entire time I had lived with her. So she tells me this movie really made her think. It occurred to her, as she said to me one night, "I need to learn how to eat raw fish, 'cause what if that happened to me? I can't just leave my Parker puppy home alone." So, one time when Mom was traveling to Baltimore on business, she met with a customer who suggested they go out with some friends for sushi and wine. Mom embraced this idea, as she just needed someone who really understood that culture—we're talking around 2005 or so. Mom had seen the movie several years earlier, but had not met anyone she could share the whole sushi experience with. Her new friends knew a lot about how to order and helped her out with making choices. Mom tells me the taste and experience was so awesome, and the wine really set the sushi off for her. At that point, she was intrigued.

The next part of this story happens four years later. My mom moved to Reunion Resort in Central Florida. She had purchased a property there in 2006 while she still owned our "ranchette" in Apopka, where I pretty much grew up with our horse, Tigger. Mom moved there because it became apparent that with the economy the way it was, something had to give. In her infinite wisdom, it occurred to her that we could rent our five-bedroom, four-acre property in Apopka as a furnished executive rental and move to Reunion to live in a three-bedroom townhouse. After all, it was on the golf course and very close to the airport, which she flew from at least three times a month, sometimes more.

Well, the property rented easily and we moved! OMG, it was so amazing, the views of nature and the openness of the property were right up my alley!

Moving is such a job. My mom had a very good friend, Michael, who helped her with the move. I like Michael; he is a sincere and dear friend to my mom! I love people that treat her with love and respect! ☺

Now here's the deal—we moved in and started to adjust. My mom had heard there was a great sushi bar, and the chef was just about the best anyone had ever seen. So once we were settled, she checked it out. When she came home after that first night of eating sushi at The Grande (a restaurant at the Reunion Resort) with Chef Ha, she just couldn't talk about anything else. I mean, seriously, it was like she was obsessed or something.

So she went to work and left me alone a lot, but when she came home from business trips, the sushi bar seemed to calm her. During this time and because of some bizarre ideas from employees at the sushi bar and others, Mom decided to write the first book, *My Wine and Sushi Diet*, as told by Parker (that's me!). The idea occurred to her in this way . . . when she walked through the front doors of The Grande, the bellmen and all the attendants would say, "Welcome back, Ms. Coons. Are you here for sushi?" And her response would be, "Yes, I'm on a wine and sushi diet." This became on ongoing mantra for my mom, as she went for sushi as often as time would allow. The idea for the book actually came from an employee at The Grande, who asked if she was considering writing a book. This had not occurred to her, and the idea seemed odd. She thought, "Who would read a book like that? What would make it stand out, to get someone's attention?" The same employee saw her again and said, "When are you writing the book?" My mom responded, "Well, this works for me, and yes, I do think it could benefit others, but I'm not sure how it would catch on." The employee said, "Why not tell it from Parker's point of view—maybe that would work." Yep, that's how it came to be . . . thanks, Peter, wherever you are these days! ☺

Now here comes the fun stuff about the Evolution! My mom says she lost between fifteen and eighteen pounds since writing the first book, which was published in February of 2011. Since that publication, she has sushi or sashimi four or five nights a week. My mom sticks to the diet and says that another great benefit is that it's fun and stress-free, which is the story of the Evolution in many ways. After my mom fell and hurt her head, she had a lot of time to evaluate her life. Lying in the hospital for three days really makes one think, she says. It turns out, when I pulled her down, I created a vertigo effect, called BPPV—Benign Paroxysmal Positional Vertigo, which happens when crystals dislodge or break in the inner ear. My mom's friend Roxanne, a massage therapist, along with her husband John, helped her discover this condition. The neurologist from the hospital believed something had happened as a result of the fall, but it took time to diagnose it properly. Thank goodness for friends! Roxanne found an ENT who specialized in the Epley maneuver, a treatment that corrected the situation immediately. This incident changed my mom's life forever. She had already begun a Master's Degree program in digital and new media marketing at Full Sail University. With that going on, it occurred to her, "Why am I battling a downturned economy in manufacturing kitchen cabinets and office furniture—although this business was so good to me for more than twenty-five years—when I could prepare myself for something new and different and transfer my skills to a field that is prospering, like resort living and hospitality?" My mom did just that.

With that said, a whole new world was born for me! Mom had a meeting with the last company she had represented out of Canada for more than nineteen years, and together they decided it was best for her to move on. She began pursuing other avenues. With seven courses of Master's work behind her, she applied to many places, including Walt Disney World and Marriott. After living in a resort for more than three years and studying the resort and hospitality industry, she recognized Marriott as the best company for whom to be employed. She also felt strongly about the possibilities with Disney. Turns out, she got a part-time job at Marriott in their marketing department. Then, in all craziness, Disney offered her a full-time professional internship. She accepted that position, and then, by the grace of God, Marriott offered her a full-time position with full benefits! So she is working at

Marriott in marketing, no weekends, and is home with me all the time.

Mom says I have to start telling stories about her now and about our general experiences living in the best resort community on earth!

So, my mom hangs out at the sushi bar in The Grande at Reunion. She even has her own seat—everyone knows where it is.

She has met and is friends with many people at the sushi bar. Some of them will appear as cartoons in this book. The first I have to start with is Chef Ha, the best sushi chef in the world, my mom says. She meets so many people from all over, and they all agree, "It is the best sushi anywhere!" How do we define good sushi, you ask? Well, all I can say is, the freshest fish, prepared in the best way, with the best presentation, and some special sauce and nothing overly fancy. That is the Chef Ha way. He is a very self-effacing man and is truly the best sushi chef ever!

Now the thing is, he couldn't get the job done at Reunion without his "Sushiteers," the servers and bartenders that get it done! They tend to everyone's needs and really appreciate Chef Ha's talents. The key to this whole crew is being humble and taking the best care of the customers, period!

Thank you!
Alex

HOPE you ENJOY YOUR STAY. :)

OMG, my mom has met so many people at Reunion and maintains many relationships, whether they are members or guests. She says we have all types, many of which will appear as characters in the next few pages. They have no names, but they are all my mom's friends.

It is really fun to enjoy life and realize the Evolution is what life is about. How many of us can say we reinvent ourselves? Somehow my mom did this. She had to deal with a failing economy, but didn't falter. Somehow she had the fortitude to go forward, with a different outlook, and change her dreams. I am certain I was a part of that decision. My love for my mom is immeasurable, and I am so very grateful she is now home regularly. She says there are some people who have been friends with her for more than four years, who really do understand the Evolution she's going through. Ellen, Steve and Sarah know her the best and have been with her through the good times and the bad, the craziness and the fun, and most of all, through the process of love and acceptance of each other without filters or walls.

Some of the people my mom meets at the sushi bar are truly characters. Some have the most unusual stories and experiences they share with her. But the most amazing occurrence while she is eating and drinking her wine at the sushi bar is that most people are at the resort to have fun.

Whether they are there on a business conference or on vacation, they are in their "fun" state. Most are relaxed and letting go of their life's troubles while at the resort.

This environment has helped my mom to experience life in a different way and led to the Evolution. Once she realized how stressful it had been to live and work for so many years in the complicated world of manufacturing, she understood the importance of living with less and having fun. She says that working for a great company that treats its employees fairly and compassionately is just unbeatable. She says it may having something to do with having represented, in her old life, up to fourteen companies at the same time, managing the business for twenty years, and dealing with all the financial strains that go with it. That lifestyle can "kill" people, whether through a health condition, a mental condition or just a crazy life. Mom has met many people at Reunion who have themselves recognized the benefits of having fun and being less stressed. Some of these characters have become her great friends through these last three years of living at the resort. Can you imagine being my mom and seeing these characters? She says these folks represent all the different people she meets at the sushi bar, complete strangers, who at the end of the day have great things in common—love for fun, love for wine or beer, love for good quality sushi and love for people. As Barbra Streisand sings, "People who need people are the luckiest people in the world." My mom feels this way about the people she meets at the resort and those who live there as members. She says that no matter what happens, they have a good time together. All I know is, I have never seen my mom as happy as she is today, and that counts for something! She refers lovingly to these newfound friends she meets every day at the sushi bar as her bobbleheads! They come from all walks of life and have such interesting conversations with her. We are grateful for such fun positive experiences in her life and we thank Chef Ha!

You know, one reason my mom began to realize something had to change in her life was when she began reflecting on her entire life and what it all meant. She had led an interesting young life, as she was raised by her grandmother, whom she called Mam-ma. She tells me Mam-ma raised her from the age of one because her mom was disabled and her father was in the military. With all the overseas travel, it was impossible for her dad to care for her mom, her brother and my mom. Mom's grandmother was a very strong woman with an independent spirit and a driven personality. But after she had a stroke at age 84, Mam-ma said to my mom, "Lisa, whatever you do, make sure you enjoy life and don't work yourself to death." Mom says the memory of her Mam-ma saying that kept resonating in her mind after the accident and while staying at home nursing her broken collarbone and struggling with vertigo. Mom takes me to Kentucky for the family reunion held every year in honor of Mam-ma. The family is awesome, the Keown Bivins Clan! Now once it became evident that life needed to change, my mom put everything in place to re-invent herself. She says there are many ways to accomplish this, one being to develop an outline to follow. I'm going to share this outline in my book, and Mom says if you just put these things in place, you can experience life-changing events.

Here goes, random thoughts from Mom:

1. Develop Positive Thinking

I put this first because I think it's the keystone habit that will help you form the other important habits. Sure, positive thinking by itself won't lead to success, but it certainly goes a long way to motivate you to do the other things required.

2. Single-tasking—the opposite of multi-tasking

You'll be more effective with your tasks and get more done. It's hard to achieve important things if you're constantly switching tasks and distracted by other *urgent* things. You'll be less stressed overall and (in my experience) happier throughout your day.

3. Focus on one goal

Just as focusing on one task at a time is more effective, and focusing on one habit at a time is more effective, so is focusing on one goal at a time. While it might seem very difficult, focusing on one goal at a time is the most powerful way of achieving your goals. When you try to take on many goals at once, you're spreading thin your focus and energy, the two critical components for achieving a goal.

What if you have five goals you want to achieve? Pick one to focus on first. If it's a longer-term goal, break it into mini-goals, then pick an action you can do today. Keep doing this until the goal is accomplished—do an action every day, finish the mini-goal, then pick the next mini-goal to work on. Then when your One Goal is completed, focus on the next one.

4. Eliminate the non-essential

First, identify the essential—the things in your life that are most important to you, that you love the most. Then eliminate everything else. This simplifies things and leaves you with the space to focus on the essential. This process works with anything—your life in general, work projects and tasks, emails and other communication. This will change your life because it will help you to simplify, to focus on what's important and to build the life you want.

5. Kindness

Yes, kindness is a habit, and it can be cultivated. Focus on it every day for a month and you'll see profound changes in your life. You'll feel better about yourself as a person. You'll see people react to you differently and treat you better over the long run. It's karma.

How do you develop the kindness habit? First, make it a goal to do something kind for someone each day. At the beginning of the day, figure out what that kind act will be, and then do it during the day. Second, each time you interact with someone, try to be kind, be friendly, be compassionate. Third, try to go beyond small kindnesses to larger acts of compassion, volunteering to help those in need and taking the initiative to relieve suffering.

6. Daily routine

It's so simple, but creating a daily routine for yourself can make a big difference in your life. The best routines, I've found, come at the start and end of the day—both your workday and your day in general. Develop a routine for when you wake, for when you first start working, for when you finish your workday and for the end of your evening. This is the hardest for me, maintaining a routine. I think it was due to all the travel for work in my life—it was so inconsistent.

How will that change your life? It will help you get a great start to your day and finish your day by preparing for the next day. It'll help you develop the productive habits you want to firm up in your everyday life. It'll help you focus on what's important, not just on what comes up. It'll help you make sure you get done all the things you really want to do everyday. And that can mean a lot.

7. Walk your dog

Seriously, walking your dog helps you think. It is a form of exercise, and it makes you feel better about yourself and more confident. That leads to better success, with other positive changes. It also helps with creativity, stress relief and confidence. Exercise is important, whether it is simply walking the dog or an all-out exercise routine.

I hope that section wasn't too deep for you all. Now we're going back to FUN! Mom says that most of all, you have to have fun, all the time! Whether you are at home, work, church, social events, charity events or sushi bars, YOU must have fun. Mom says this entails **laughing**! You see, when you are laughing and playing, you are having FUN! Mom says to watch for the

FUN POLICE! They are everywhere, and if they are not, then you are not having FUN! Mom learns this from me too, 'cause I have fun playing with my toys all the time! She says once you can take the outline above and have FUN with it, then you are on the track to enjoying life and not being too SERIOUS! Yikes, I don't know how to be serious—I like being a dog!! ☺

Part of the fun for Mom is playing golf. Again, this is one of the main reasons she bought our place. An LPGA tournament at Reunion brought her there, and her love of golf is why she is going to live and retire there. Now that she doesn't have to travel all over the place, she can spend more time playing golf with her friends! Yay! Many of the members play with Mom, and she also likes to play with family and friends. Watch out, world, Mom will be on the course more often! She says it one of the most relaxing and fun thing she does. I can imagine it—I like chasing balls too! ☺

Oh yeah, once in awhile, before the golfers are on the course, I get to walk there and check it out. What a beautiful place!

Looks like we are near the conclusion of

the Evolution. As you will see, in the next part of this book are the contents of my first book, which includes all the elements of my mom's Wine and Sushi Diet. If you bought the first book, this next section is a replica. The first book is no longer available from the book stores, as all of the original content is now in this one. We hope you enjoy the actual diet, as this is how we have so much fun!! For healthy meal tips when not eating sushi, check out my new friends Bren Ankrum - Culinary Editor and Donna Hargrove - Nutrition Editor and their website: NutritionHealthNet.com

My Wine and Sushi Diet—as told by Parker

My mom and I live at a place called Reunion Resort. Reunion is a golf community in central Florida, about fifty miles from Apopka, where I used to live, and about thirty minutes south of Orlando, and twenty-five minutes from Orlando International Airport.

Reunion is next to Disney World, where the entire world goes to escape life's realities and take their families on the greatest vacations of all, or so they say. I wouldn't know, because I've never been there☺—no dogs allowed, unless you are a service dog (*wonder if my mom could get me in training?*). My vacations take place when someone comes over to take care of me while my mom is traveling on business and stays away days at a time. Now sometimes I travel with her when she works in the Carolinas. We stay a week! Woo Hoo!

I was born in Winter Park, Florida, and had three siblings, as far as I can remember. The day I met my mom, everything changed. I saw her, licked her nose, and that was that. I went to live with her! Somehow I came to live in Altamonte Springs, then in Apopka.

My mom bought a horse, Tigger, and life became very, very interesting at that point. I learned how to stay out of Tigger's way and to chase rats at the barn! My life would soon become very different, as my mom has included me in all her life adventures . . .

You see, I am Parker, and, well . . . somehow my mom thinks I can write this book about her diet, THE WINE and SUSHI DIET. I love my mom, so here goes:

Mom says the first thing you need is to be recovering from a crisis of some sort in your life. You have to be in a place of, well, not despair, but some sort of beginning to redefine your life. You need a constant, if at all possible, someone like me. Someone who always loves you, wherever we are, whatever we are doing, whomever we are with!

Day 1

Dinner (never after 8 pm)

One roll of sushi and two glasses of wine. Before that, beer at four o'clock is okay—that's what Doris says. (More about her later.) Also, Mom says if you don't like raw fish, eat California rolls or tempura shrimp rolls with steamed shrimp on the outside of the wrap.

Now of course you'll want other meals, when you can choose to eat yogurt, blueberries, turkey, cheese and milk.

Might be a good idea to have the yogurt for breakfast with the blueberries, and the turkey, cheese and milk for lunch. Ooooops! Forgot the coffee . . . two cups each morning, no matter what!!

The key to The Wine and Sushi Diet is to eat the best sushi ever, which is at Reunion Resort in the lobby bar (according to Mom). Chef Michael Ha is the best ever, and the bartenders, Lisa, Ryan, Tanya and Alex, are awesome! Chef Michael makes the best sushi my mom has had anywhere, and she should know—she eats it everywhere. She especially likes the Grande Reunion Roll, which is the tempura shrimp style I referred to earlier. Also, my mom says that sushi, wherever you eat it, has to be very, very fresh and well prepared. She says this is crucial to the diet's success!!

Sometimes her really good friends, Ellen, Sarah and Steve, drive to Reunion just to eat sushi because it is soooo good!

DAY 2: Same thing, just a different day

DAY 3: On day three, it's a good idea to eat something different. If you don't, you might get sick of sushi at this point. My mom says no red meat, period! I think she knows what she's talking about, 'cause she hasn't eaten any in twenty-five years. She is fifty-six. Also, she said that on Day 3, I should tell you more about her. AND why this diet is working for her.

My mom loves to have fun and works hard to do so. When we are home, we enjoy our private time together. She travels a lot and arranges people to dog-sit me. I think that is pretty cool.

My mom has worked all her life; she graduated from college in October of 1977 and went to work the very next day as a speech therapist for schoolchildren. After three years of that, she traveled to Florida on spring break with a friend, fell in love with the area, was offered a job in a local school system and moved!

The rest is Coons history. After a year in the Florida school system, she went into sales. Ten years later, she started her own manufacturer's representative agency and has been in sales for a total of thirty years. For twenty years she managed her own business, which is why I am writing this book, so my mom can retire and stay home with me more!! (Wouldn't that be something?☺)

Okay, she says back to the diet stuff!

Day 4: MORE sushi today! One roll of sushi, two glasses of wine, and some sashimi! And of course, still eating blueberries and yogurt, plus granola for breakfast and a tuna sandwich for lunch. And beer at 4:00 pm. That's what Doris says. Mom says I need to tell you about Doris on Day 4.

Doris, hmmmm . . . Well, my mom met Doris, who is seventy-nine years old now, thirteen years ago. Doris was sixty-six and was riding a motorcycle, ALL the time, everywhere. She rides from Florida to Canada every summer and is a member of the Motor Maids. Check them out at www.motormaids.org! It is the first and oldest continuously operated women's motorcycle riding organization! In 1940, it was established as a women's motorcycling organization in North America. The Motor Maids are pioneers, and since my mom has felt like a pioneer all her life, she joined them. My mom always viewed her grandmother as a pioneer and she says she has turned out like her to some pretty large degree. She thinks that is a good thing! Mom says it was here she learned how to laugh, play and really enjoy life! Doris has been a good friend to me; she stays with me a lot when Mom travels. I love Doris and the Motor Maids!

Day 5: Mom says this is a very fun day of the diet. On this day you can eat PASTA! Yep, pasta . . . that defies all the diet theories, doesn't it? Oh, well, my mom has never been conventional! She says we need to talk about exercise on Day 5.

Exercise is a must when you're on The Wine and Sushi Diet. You need to walk your dog every day for a minimum of three miles: one and a half miles in the morning and one and a half miles in the afternoon.

Well, at least thirty minutes a day, twice a day! If you don't have a dog, maybe you should go to the pound and get one, or find someone selling puppies on the curb, like my mom found me! It's much more fun to walk with your dog than to walk alone or even with a human. You don't have to carry on a conversation; therefore you don't have to think. You just get to enjoy the beauty of the land. As Doris says, take a walkabout!

DAY 6: Now on Day 6, since you have had four days of sushi, you can either eat sushi or not. Mom recommends you do eat sushi, as you are more likely to lose weight faster. She also says that on Day 6 I should tell you that you could cut back to one glass of wine if you want. Also, Mom says if you drink more than two glasses of wine or more than one beer a day, you will probably not lose weight very fast! This is an FYI, just so you don't have unrealistic expectations.

DAY 7: The day of rest. This is a day you can rest and not do anything. You can take your dog on short walks, so business gets taken care of. ☺ Maybe consider sitting

outside in the sun and reading a book. Of course you need to eat, **but you can eat anything you want**, as long as you **don't go over 1500 calories.** This is the only day you need to think about calories, because you are not eating sushi. Just remember, if you drink beer or wine on the seventh day, you have to count the calories!

After you have done this fun diet—actually, I call it a "lifestyle"—you can start thinking about some other foods and their healthiness. My mom did some research on hypoglycemic foods. Here she wants me to list the good vs. the not-good foods, to help with your new diet lifestyle.

She learned about this by going to the website http://commonsensehealth.com, where she found the lists below.

Two simple categories of glycemic foods make choosing easier.

- "Foods to Refuse" are high-glycemic and/or unhealthy.
- "Foods to Choose" are healthy low-glycemic foods.

Protein Foods to Choose

Choose these foods baked, broiled, grilled or steamed.

Beef, ground (<10% fat)

Beef, lean cuts

Calamari

Chicken, skinless

Clams

Crabs

Mussels

Octopus

Oysters

Pork, trimmed

Rabbit

Scallops

Fish (fresh or frozen)	Shrimp
Fish (canned in water)	Tofu
Ham, lean	Tuna (canned in water)
Lamb, lean	Turkey
Lobster	Venison

Protein Foods to Refuse

Refuse breaded, fried, deep-fried or sautéed foods.

Bacon	Jerky (beef/turkey)
Beef, fatty cuts	Liver
Beef, ground (>10% fat)	Liverwurst
Canadian bacon	Pepperoni
Chicken (fried and/or with skin)	Salami
Chicken (buffalo wings)	Sausage
Duck	Seafood (canned in oil)

Fish sticks

Hot dogs (pork, beef, turkey, chicken)

Turkey bacon

Turkey sausage

Vegetables to Choose

Choose baked, boiled, broiled, raw or steamed.

Artichokes (and hearts)

Asparagus

Bamboo shoots

Okra

Olives

Onion

Bean sprouts

Palm hearts

Beans (green, wax)

Peas

Bok Choy

Peppers (all types)

Broccoli

Pickles (dill)

Cabbage

Purslane

Carrots, raw

Radishes

Cauliflower

Rutabagas

Celery

Snow Peas

Chilies

Soybeans

Cucumbers

Eggplant

Greens (spinach, chard, kale)

Jicama

Leeks

Lettuce

Mushrooms

Squash (all except pumpkin)

Tomato sauce, paste

Tomatoes

Water chestnuts

Zucchini

Soup (broth & listed veggies)

Vegetables to Refuse

Avoid breaded, fried, deep fried or sautéed foods.

Avocados

Beets

Carrots (cooked)

Pickles (sweet)

Potatoes(all types)

Pumpkin

Corn

Sweet potatoes

Olives (packed in oil)

Sweet relish

Parsnips

Yams

Fruits to Choose

Apple

Orange

Apricots

Blueberries

Blackberries

Cantaloupe

Cherries

Grapefruit

Grapes (all types)

Honeydew

Kiwi

Melon

Palmello

Papaya

Peach

Pear

Pineapple

Plum

Raspberries

Strawberries

Tangelo

Tangerine

Nectarine

Watermelon

Fruits to Refuse

Bananas

Candied fruit

Coconut

Dates

Dried fruit

Fruit sauces

Mangoes

Marmalade

Persimmons

Plantains

Fruit juices

Raisins

Fruit preserves

Breads and Cereals to Choose

100% sprouted wheat

Whole grain

100% whole wheat

Unsweetened bran cereals

Multi-grain

Muesli (low fat, no sugar

	added)
Oat bran bread	Oat bran
Pita, whole wheat	Oats, oatmeal
Pumpernickel	Puffed wheat (unsweetened)
Rye	Rice bran

Breads and Cereals to Refuse

Bagels (all types)	English muffins

Biscuits

Bread (except those on "Choose" list)

Bread crumbs

Bread sticks

Cakes

Cereal (except those on "Choose" list)

Chips (all types)

Granola (all types)

Melba toast

Muffins (all types)

Pancakes

Pastries (all types)

Pita bread (white)

Popcorn

Cookies	Popcorn cakes
Cornbread	Rice cakes
Crackers (all types)	Rolls (dinner, hamburger buns, etc.)
Croissants	Tortillas (except whole wheat)
Donuts	Waffles

Starchy Foods to Choose

Barley

Beans (black, kidney, red, garbanzo, etc.)

Buckwheat

Bulgur

Chickpeas

Lentils

Oats, oatmeal

Pasta, whole wheat

Peas (split, black-eyed)

Rice (basmati, bulgur, brown, wild)

Couscous

Tabouli

Dahl

Starchy Foods to Refuse

Beans (baked, refried)

Pretzels

Granola (all types)

Rice (white, fried, Spanish)

Noodles, ramen-style

Soups (all types except

	vegetable broth)
Pasta (white, green, red)	Taco shells
Potatoes (all types)	

Dairy Foods to Choose

Cheese (fat-free or low-fat)	Mozzarella cheese (fat-free)
Cottage cheese (low-fat)	

	Ricotta cheese (fat-free)
Eggs, egg whites (no added fat)	Tempeh
Egg substitute	Tofu
Milk (1% low-fat, fat-free)	Yogurt (low-fat, fat-free, sugar-free)

Dairy Foods to Refuse

Cheese (except those on "Choose" list)

Cottage cheese (full-fat)

Cream / half & half

Cream cheese (all types)

Frozen yogurt

Ice cream

Milk (whole, 2% fat)

Mozzarella (full-fat)

Sorbet (all types)

Sour cream (full-fat)

Yogurt (full-fat)

Beverages to Choose

Water (mineral, sparkling, sugar-free)	Sugar-free beverages
Bouillon	Hot cocoa (sugar-free, fat-free)
Coffee (no sugar, fat-free milk)	Tea (all types, no sugar)

Diet soda

Beverages to Refuse

Alcohol (beer, wine, mixed drinks)

Beverages with sugar, high-fructose corn syrup or other caloric sweeteners

Sweets and Treats to Choose

Diet soda

Sugar-free

popsicles

Sugar-free gelatin

Sugar-free pudding

Non-nutritive natural or artificialsweeteners

Sweets and Treats to Refuse

Candy bars

Molasses

Chocolates

Frozen treats (with sugar)

Honey	Soda (with sugar)
Jam/jelly	Syrup (all types)
Marmalade	Tofu frozen dessert

Condiments to Choose

Butter (1 pat per day)	Olives (packed in

	water)
Butter substitute (1 pat per day)	Onion
Garlic	Parmesan cheese (1 Tbsp./day)
Ginger	Romano cheese (1 Tbsp./day)
Herbs	Pickles (dill)
Horseradish	Salad dressing (lo-cal, fat-free)

Hummus

Ketchup (1 Tbsp./day)

Lemon juice

Lime juice

Margarine (1 pat per day)

Mayonnaise (light/fat-free, 1 Tbsp./day)

Mustard (lo-cal)

Oil (olive)

Salsa (4 Tbsp./day)

Sauerkraut

Shallots

Sour cream(low-fat, fat-free)

Soy sauce

Spaghetti sauce (sugar-free)

Spices (all)

Tahini sauce

Condiments to Refuse

Bacon bits	Salad dressings (full-fat)
Croutons	Sandwich spreads
Lard	Seeds (sunflower, pumpkin, etc.)

Mayonnaise (full fat)

Olives (packed in oil)

Peanut butter

Pickles (except dill)

Shortening (vegetable)

Sour cream (full-fat)

Sweet pickle relish

Now I say, Mom, you can't be serious! These experts say don't drink wine or any alcohol! Well, here is my mom's philosophy: if you have to choose a poison, her choice is wine and beer (occasionally), a martini a time or two, and of course, margaritas on rare occasions. She says this is the only diet she ever had fun with and allowed her to lose weight gradually. It depended on her exercise, to be honest—thus, more walks!

Oh, wait—I forgot something. My mom got really sick in January this year with that flu bug going around. So guess what she did? She bought a Jack LaLanne Juicer! Yes, I couldn't believe it. She hates the kitchen, but one morning she came dragging in here with bags full of fresh fruits and vegetables. I couldn't believe it—I never see her do anything in the kitchen except occasionally use the microwave. Hmmm, I said to myself, why are you acting so weird?

Well, the next thing I knew, she turned this machine on, it was kinda loud, and then she started throwing these fresh fruits and vegetables in there. Holy cow, stuff went flying everywhere, apples on my bed and blueberries on my head! It was crazy!

I said, you can't be serious? This is gonna help you—what about me? I can't be a garbage can! Well, it turns out, she forgot to put on the back of the unit that catches the waste. Pretty funny!

I can't take it anymore right now, but I sure hope you have as much fun with this as my mom is!

And we hope it works for you. Just follow this Wine and Sushi Diet every week for a year, and you may lose weight. If you don't, at least it was fun trying and fun looking at the pictures in this book and learning about ME, Parker, and wine and sushi!

PARKER

Made in the USA
Charleston, SC
01 December 2012